POSTCARDS FROM GREECE
AND OTHER POEMS
NEMONE LETHBRIDGE

NEMONE LETHBRIDGE

Nemone Lethbridge has asserted her rights to be identified as the author of this work in accordance with Section 77 of the Copyright, Designs and Patents Act 1988

All rights reserved. No part of this publication may be reproduced, stored in a retrieval system or transmitted in any form or by any means, electronic, mechanical, photocopying or otherwise, without the prior written consent of the publisher.

2nd edition Milo O'Connor 2022
First published 2021

Enquires milo.oconnor@outlook

Cover Design : lissak.com

© 2022 Nemone Lethbridge

These poems were written over a period of fifty years. They are intended to complement my autobiography **Nemone.**

DEDICATION
ON FLOWERS BROUGHT TO MY MOTHER.
IN MEMORIAM.

The mist has muffled all the valley,
And languid is the rise
Of bonfire smoke towards the pigeon-grey
Of September skies:
The fly-blown blackberries sprawl each meadow's edge,
And burden every hedge.

I came upon the saffron marching
A corps in spectre-blue:
I loved that army on the hillside,
And so I bring to you
Twelve blooms more mournful than a purple cloud,
One whiter than a shroud.

INDEX

1 Ares Hill

2 Ayios Elias

3 A Sceptic Surveys some Minor Saints of the Orthodox Calendar

4 On the Secret Shore

5 An English School Teacher Surveys

6 Two Islands

7 Traffic Jam

8 Astinonemea

9 The Ship of Fools

10 A Rent Boy's Song

11 Yesterday's Ravers

12 Mykonos

IN TIMES OF WAR AND HARDSHIP

13 Holy Land

14 Isis

15 Aleppo

16 A Refugee Remembers

17 Tunde the African

18 Holocaust

19 Lucy and Perpetua

20 Haile Selassie

TWO DANISH SEASCAPES

21

(i) Kerteminde
(ii) Elsinore

TRANSLATIONS

22 Sonnet after Ronsard "Ces longues nuicts d'hyver"
23 Variations on St John of the Cross
(i)   Strange Birds
(ii) Madonna of the Winter Flowers

MISCELLANEOUS POEMS 1954 TO DATE

24 Oxford Trinity Term 1954
25 A View of the Potteries
26 Love on the Southern Region
27 Damage Barton
28 Dash

TRANSGENERATIONAL

Poems written by my mother and youngest grandson.

29 Freda - Katharine Lethbridge 1904 – 2001.
30 The Sprite - Caleb O'Connor written age 10
31 The Battle of Hastings - Caleb O'Connor   written age 12

EPILOGUE

32 Nativity

NEMONE LETHBRIDGE

POSTCARDS FROM GREECE

ARES HILL
ACTS CHAPTER 17
VERSES 21, 22, 23

21. For all the Athenians and strangers which were there spent their time in nothing else but either to tell or to hear some new thing.

22. Then Paul stood in the midst of Ares Hill and said: "Ye men of Athens, I perceive that in all things you are somewhat superstitious

23. For as I passed by and beheld your devotions, I found an altar with this inscription 'To the unknown god'.

    Men of Athens sceptic heard
    The Pauline preaching of the Word –
    Resolving when the Saint had spoken
    To keep their pious options open –
    Rechiselled in the burning stone
    "To the Unknown God – (or a god unknown)".

    Ye Men of Athens! Still you walk
    And send the sun down with your talk;
    Dialectic still you meet
    And argue in each darkening street;
    When times are bad each you placate
    Olympian goddess, Christian saint.

AYIOS ELIAS

Great Mount Elias, from your savage peak
Darkly elyptical from pole to pole
We see the blue Aegean and Ionian role,
The smoking sunset and the smoking freak.
The long escarpment conquered, strive to speak:
"What is this place? And where its secret soul?
Fragmented Hellas, strive to make us whole.
Holy Byzantine, wily sceptic Greek."
The Turks have gone and now the tourists come.
Dubious the parts, corrupt the total sum.
Silent the seas, detergent white the foam;
Adulterous Helen – can you call us home?
Great Mount Elias! When all's said and done
Elijah, are you? Or the mighty sun?

A SCEPTIC SURVEYS SOME
MINOR SAINTS OF THE ORTHODOX CALENDAR

<u>Ayos Sostis</u> who are you?
Who's your father?
What's he do?
I don't reckon your paternity
You look a dodgy one to me.
<u>Holy Friday</u>! What a name
You carry to eternal fame
Holy nothing! I would vote
You're nothing but a billy goat.
<u>Goody No-Shoes</u>, give me proof
That you are more than horn and hoof.

<u>Saint Dimitra</u>, where you pass
The lark leaps from the burning grass
Soft your feet have touched the fields
Till every stone a harvest yields
Corn goddess we kiss your feet
And every kiss you turn to wheat.

Pantheon and Galaxy
Panaghia and Trinity
Ayo Sosti, pray for me.

Holy Friday: Ayos Kyriakos
Goody No Shoes: "Ayos Anargiros"
"The shoe less ones": Title given to both Saint Cosmos
and Saint Damian, patrons of the medical profession
Saint Dimitra: Saint or Goddess?

ON THE SECRET SHORE

STO PERIGIALI TO KRIFO

FROM THE GREEK BY GEORGE SEFERIS, SET TO MUSIC BY MIKIS THEODORAKIS

Blazing at midday stretched the secret shore
Dove-white those sands, untrod before;
We searched for water, for we had no wine
And on our bitter tongues it turned to brine.

How blond the sea-shore where we wrote her name,
How soon the wind of morning came –
One breath had swept her name away
And sighing passed across the bay.

We saw the life we hated with clear sight,
Refused it, as the dawn the night.
Oh wind that blew across the secret bay
Oh your soft wings you carried day.

During the Greek Civil War a group of soldiers came to a lonely beach where they traced the name "Irene" (which means peace) on the sand. After a moment the waves came and washed it away.

AN ENGLISH SCHOOL TEACHER SURVEYS THE PHALLUS OF DELOS

Burning stubble, burning grass
Leave the children, leave the class
Spock and Froebel, go away
Montessori's had her day.

Pythian he calls across the sand
The marble thigh is hot to hand;
Till annular he breaks the waves
The dolphin in the deep sea caves.

TWO ISLANDS, ASSUMPTION,
15 AUGUST ANY YEAR.

Tinos

The gypsy woman cried to the Immaculate Mother of God
"Let him speak, let him hear, let him see, let him live!"
And a thousand black shawls crawled up the hill on their knees.

Mykonos

On an island nearby they were keeping vigil as well.
But no one observed Panaghia streak through the sky like a jet.
Aphrodite had rapt them, there on the beach,
Soon to bowl in on her shell.

"Panaghia"- Greek Orthodox title for the Mother of God.

On the feast of the Assumption of Our Lady to Heaven, 15 August, thousands of pilgrims converge on the basilica on the island of Tinos which houses an icon of the Virgin reputedly painted by St Luke. The occasion has an added patriotic significance as it marks the anniversary of the sinking of the pilgrim ship "Elli" by Mussolini in 1940 and the entry of Greece into the Second World War.

The pilgrims crawl the last thousand yards of the journey from harbour to basilica on their knees. This island is the equivalent of Catholic Lourdes but in the Orthodox tradition.

Mykonos is an island with a strong pagan tradition. Even in the 1960s two beaches, Paradise and Super Paradise, were nudist and full of drugs. I remember seeing a thousand naked freaks gazing out to sea as though they were waiting for something miraculous to happen. I thought of Botticelli's "Birth of Venus".

TRAFFIC JAM

I fuck your candle, brother –
I've had your Mary, said the other.
The Three-in-One I've Sod –
I've Italianised your god.
Out fell the freaks
In their oily batiques
Till the hash on the air
Cut the Ambre Solaire:
Where the wild goats once sprung
A cash computer rung.

When the people of Mykonos swear, they swear with a vengeance, combining obscenity with blasphemy. I asked my friend Hazel Fouskis to translate what two drivers were shouting at each other on the road to Ano Mera. This is the result. Hazel is an English woman who married a Greek some fifty years ago and is well versed in Mykonian dialect.

ASTINONEMEA

A policeman's lot is a happy one
On special patrol for tit and bum
With our grim black glasses to our snow-white jeep
Let each trafficker tremble and naturist weep!
Off we go to Paradise Beach
To capture the prettiest freak in reach
A crafty smoke behind the rocks
A canny check-up against the pox:
Oh we're the lads who love our work
Oh we're the lads who'll never shirk
A policeman's lot is a glorious one
On special patrol for tit and bum.

Every young policeman longed to be recruited to the Mykonos vice patrol during the sixties and seventies.

THE SHIP OF FOOLS

The Captain was smoking a joint
As we bowled round Paradise Point:
The mate was dead drunk
Asleep in his bunk.
The nude of the day
Is drenched in salt spray
While yesterday's nude
Hungover, subdued –
While the pooves in the stern
Anoint their sunburn.
Who cares if she sinks
If we salvage the drinks?
Oh! The scene is too manic
On the new-style Titanic.

Chorus of FREAKS
Rolling home! Rolling home across the sea!
Rolling home from Elia, forty thousand freaks and me!

YESTERDAY'S RAVERS

Sally Lou came from Detroit
Where they make motor cars:
Serious, high-minded, clean-living
Not much given
To hanging about it bars,
But it wasn't enough to save her
Under Aegean stars.

Twenty years' hard labour he gave her
At the top of the donkey track
And a paraffin lamp and a yawning well
And a child who finally drowned in the well
And a crown of thorns to her back.

Sally-Ann came from Luton
The story was much the same;
Ingrid from Copenhagen
Knew the self-same pain:
Twenty years at the top of the track
Varicose veins, black shawl on her back
While Odysseus played the field.

Three high minded ladies
Sixty years as slaves
But sixty years seems half-a-day
Swimming in those eyes of grey
Austere-eyed the goddess
Rising from the waves.

*Foreign girls who married local boys led a
life which was far from idyllic.*

RENT BOY'S SONG

Mr Cohn (or Mr Schine)
Oh how I wish that you were mine!
McCarthy's left hand and his right,
His anchor and his acolyte,
Commie's scourge and Liberal's terror
Pity those you catch in error.
With slicked back hair and well-cut suits
Two Bible bashing handsome brutes.
Republicans, the nation's good
The straightest men in Hollywood.

But when you go on holiday
Ah then you teach the plebs to play.
Sodom's happy hordes delight
When I become your catamite.
On Mykonos, beyond the bay
In your white jeep we'll roar away.
Oh Mr Cohn (or Mr Schine)
Ah then at last I'll know you're mine.

During the enquiry into "un-American activities" conducted by Senator McCarthy, two young attorneys named Cohn and Schine became notorious for their aggressive questioning of witnesses. During winters in New York,

Roy Cohn escorted several high-profile women, including

Barbra Streisand. During frequent summer visits to Mykonos, he was a leading member of the gay scene, well known for his white jeep and blond companions. Later he worked for Donald Trump. He died of AIDS in 1986

MYKONOS

This is the house that I built
This is the place I longed to live,
White as frost on a field of brown
A beacon for that pirate town
Whose labyrinthine streets conceal
The spoils of ancient piracy.

This is the island that I loved
This is the place I yearned to be;
Melteme swept, the bone white hill
Refracts the azure canopy,
While, far below, the tiny ships
Transnavigate the ruffled sea.

This is the garden that we made
This is the dream we dreamed and lost.
Amaranthine in the shade
These are the flowers that could not last.
That was the dream that we betrayed
Ephemeral, it bloomed and passed.

IN TIMES OF WAR AND HARDSHIP

HOLY LAND

In Jerusalem the golden
With milk and honey blest
The diggers smash the houses
The homeless get no rest.

In Bethlehem the blessed
That little starlit town
The stranger gets no welcome
They knocked the stable down.

On Golgotha, as usual,
They ply a hideous trade;
Stabat Mater Dolorosa
As when Jesus was betrayed.

Ref. "Stabat Mater", medieval Latin poem describing the suffering of the Mother of God as she stood at the foot of the cross.

ISIS

The devil stalks the desert sands,
The Satanists erect a cross;
The nails bisecting feet and hands
Demonstrate compassion's loss.

The hostage writhing in the cage
Bears witness to mankind's disgrace,
Until his spirit struggles free
And soars to interstellar space:

Through ice blue ether liberate,
Extravagant, he races free,
Till on our Mother's gentle breast
He sleeps for all eternity.

*In memoriam Menath Moaz al-Kassabeh, a Jordanian
pilot, held hostage and murdered by I.S. Syria 2015*

ALEPPO

Light's abode, celestial Salem,
Every tower is tipped with gold
Pellucid river, crystal fountain
Eden's glory manifold.

Lamb and lion lie down together
Basking in eternal sun;
Wolf cubs in that halcyon weather
Among the lilies frisk and run.

The cockatrice forgoes his venom
Gathers honey with the bees,
While the scorpion harvests nectar
From the blossom laden trees.

Blessed home, celestial Salem,
A little child shall lead the flock;
Nightingale and lark ascending
Join the shepherd on the rock.

Ruined home, extinguished Salem,
Drones are prowling overhead,
Barrel bombs have smashed the towers,
Crystal fountains running red.
By the foul polluted river
The little child is lying dead.

Verse 1   "Light's abode" opening lines of an old German hymn attributed to Thomas a Kempis."

Verses 2-3 ref. Isaiah chapter 11 verses 6 – 8

Verse 3   ref. (music) Vaughan Williams
(The Lark Ascending)
Schubert (The Shepherd on the Rock)

A REFUGEE REMEMBERS HIS GARDEN

Miraculous, the lemon tree
Is hung with blossom and with fruit.
Wax white bloom and yellow orb
Together crown each verdant shoot.
Sweet days gone in Syria.

Beyond the garden wall, the years
Relentless sweep our lives away;
All our pleading all our tears
Cannot delay them for a day.

Palmyra glistens in the sun
Where Roman sentries vigil kept;
Where fearsome hoplites battles won,
Aurelian triumphed and Zenobia wept.

Crusader castles, Papal wars
Defied the might of Saladin;
Indifferent, the frosty stars
Observe our heartbreak and our sin.

Simultaneous on the bough
Spring and Autumn days combine;
Silver and gold the lemon tree
Green malachite the fecund vine.
Once, long ago, this plot was mine.
Sweet days gone in Syria.

Aurelian, Roman Emperor, captured the city of Palmyra 273 BC and enslaved Zenobia, its Queen. In our garden in Greece the citrus trees bore fruit and flowers at the same time.

TUNDE

Tunde the African,
Naked as a flame,
Fished the gleaming river
Raced the windswept plain,
Embraced his sunlit Eden
Until the slavers came.

A slave in Mississippi
He bore his master's chain,
By the cotton fields of Babylon
He knew the exile's pain,
Dreaming of the homeland
He would never see again.

Tunde the soldier
Was buried far from home;
The clouds that glower on Dartmoor
Watched him die alone,
The rain that pelts on Dartmoor
Washed his soul away
To the sun soaked plains of Africa
Where he sleeps till judgment day.

In the war of 1812 – 1814 between the United Kingdom and the United States, over six thousand American soldiers were captured by the British. Many were incarcerated in Dartmoor Gaol. Princetown village, where the prison is located, at 1500 feet above sea level, is the highest and wettest village in Great Britain. When the war ended with *the Treaty of Ghent the white prisoners were repatriated while the Afro-Americans (numbering about one thousand) were sold by the United States to Britain for $1,204,960.*

HOLOCAUST

Rachel née Rabinovitch
Cannot shift that stubborn stain,
Nor all the soap in Stamford Hill
Exorcise tumescent pain.

In excelsis through the night
We heard the bells of Cracow ring
A Christian new year, calm and bright
Rung in by Jewish seraphim

Transtellar choruses above
Obscenity confront below;
The shuffling monster fouls the earth
And desecrates the pristine snow.

What requiem can bleach the stain
What obsequies remove the dread?
What pious rituals remain
For coffinless, for unschuled dead?

*Rachel née Rabinovitch ref. Sweeney among
the Nightingales, T.S. Eliot 1920*

In 1974, when I moved to North London, I made friends with the manageress of Grodzinski's baker's shop, a refugee from Nazi occupied Poland. She told me how, after a massacre in her village, it had been impossible to dig graves because the earth was frozen solid. The dead were buried under the snow.

LUCY AND PERPETUA

Lucy and Perpetua
Two little Roman girls
Camellia faces, burnished hair
In artificial curls.

Wealthy and patrician
With Olympian gifts endowed,
Venus gave them beauty
Juno made them proud.
With Daddy in the Senate
One's status is assured,
With Daddy rich as Croesus
"How come one is so bored?"

Marriages had been arranged
Dowries fixed upon,
Each glossy Roman virgin
A trophy to be won.

Each little Roman madam
Like a spoilt brat behaves,
Teasing her admirers
Tormenting the slaves;
Rejecting her poor suitors
Each ruined Roman child
"Shows no consideration"
Drives her parents wild.

But whence comes this clap of thunder
This terrifying love
When Christ the Galilean

Sweeps earthwards from above?

Lucy and Perpetua
Threw their lives away:
In the nightmare of the circus
Chose to spend their wedding day.

Triumphantly, in glory
They ascend to martyrs' thrones;
While crocodile and leopard
Gnaw their pearl white bones.

"*cum Felicitate Perpetua, Agatha, Lucia, Agnate, Caecelia, Anastasia et omnibus Sanctis tuis: intra nos consortium, non aestimator meriti, sed veniae, quaesumus, largitor admitte. Per Christum Dominum nostrum.*"

"*with Lucy and Perpetua and all thy saints. Into their company we pray thee to admit us, not weighing our deserts but freely granting us forgiveness: through Christ our Lord.*"

(From the Canon of the Mass.)

HAILE SELASSIE

Last year he wore a golden crown
Lion of Judah, King of Kings;
Nations trembled at his frown,
Laid at his feet their offerings

Now small and hunched the Emperor walks
A refugee in English rain,
On his weary back he bears
The burden of his people's pain.

Last year she wore a sparkling gown,
The little skinny black Princess;
Today a gymslip made of serge
And a cosy chill-proof vest.

Last year the Emperor instructs
His child in global politics;
Today she's giggling in the dorm
And playing jolly hockey sticks.

These are the lodgings where he slept
The chilly park bench where he sat.
The Lion of Judah has become
An English pussy cat.

When Mussolini invaded Abyssinia in 1935 Emperor Haile Selassie addressed The League of Nations in Geneva appealing for help for his country. No one came forward. The Emperor went into exile in England and his little daughter went to Bath High School. His followers, the Rastafarians, believe that he is the direct descendant of Solomon and the Queen of Sheba, that he is still alive and he will come one day and reclaim his throne.

TWO DANISH SEASCAPES
Written at the launching of the oil
tanker Dorthe Maersk, August 1954
For Emma and Maersk Mckinney Møller

(i) KERTEMINDE

Annular, cold harbour, circled agate:
Motionless the water by the quay,
Unsplintered by the mast of frozen frigate,
Untroubled by the wind that stirs the sea
Beyond the bar with curls of ruffled plumage,
And sings unnoticed its sardonic runes –
Strange flotsam, unexamined wreckage,
The whimpering betrayal of the dunes;

But, when a bird's cold cry first startles April,
It wakes a crew long sleeping underground,
Once more the proud keel grates the icy shingle
And feels the urgent bucking of the sound:
For happy Leif must seek his new world's gold –
Oh laughing finder, who forgot to hold!

Leif Ericson, aka Leif the lucky, a Viking, landed on the coast of

North America some five hundred years before Columbus

(ii) ELSINORE

The pale intoxication of the Northern night,
Where sunset and the pewter dawn are one,
Where phosphorescent waves refract the light
And mock the castle's dark obsidian,
Shall, sweeping with the crescent tide's advance,
Submerge our sorrow with the salt sea-wrack,
Shall beat along the blood of those that dance
Along the shore of shining Skagerrak;

Oh drain the fiery chalice to the end,
Nor, in its brief enchantment, care to know
How soon the traitor mistletoe must bend
To bring the pride of golden Baldur low;
Nor, turning slowly southwards, care to mark
The snuffed-out candelabra of the dark.

Baldur "the beautiful" who symbolized light and virtue, was murdered by his blind brother Hodur who symbolized darkness and evil, using a weapon made from a sprig of mistletoe.

TRANSLATIONS

SONNET
AFTER "CES LONGUES NUITS D'HYVER" BY RONSARD. (FROM THE FRENCH)

When through the boredom of a winter's night
The dawdling moon has slouched her listless way,
The cock unhurriedly calls up the day
Disconsolate, and in the wan cold light;

How could I live without the dim delight
Your lips afford, perfume of night's bouquet;
You sleep: I dream that you are mine alway
Caught in the velvet subterfuge of night –

Forgetting that you never were my own,
Forgetting how the heart must love alone,
Oh lovely lie, deception most divine;

For though your own sweet flesh desire redeemed,
Yet you may never know how I have dreamed
That your abstracted pilgrim soul was mine.

VARIATIONS ON A THEME OF ST JOHN OF THE CROSS.
(FROM THE SPANISH)
i STRANGE BIRDS

Beyond the poverty
Of winter's hushed and unresponsive grey,
With dreamer's clarity
I saw them far away –
White birds that wheeled and flashed above their prey.

Oh diamond in the dark,
Oh swift negation of the winter's pain,
Oh wheeling birds that mark
The clouds, pregnant with rain,
With searing lights of Pentecostal flame!

But, as I watched, they turned
Upon the swift enchantment of their flight,
Like August lightning burned,
A shimmer of delight,
And then had darted down the gulf of night.

As Orpheus dared the shade
And starless night of Orcus to recover
The golden Thracian maid,
Eurydice, lost lover,
So, loving, raked I chaos to discover
The place where they had flown,
And in their joyous errand had alighted:
And yet I searched alone,

No flash of wing delighted
That void between the whimpering worlds benighted.

Oh darkness of that void,
Oh dawning after darkness more divine:
I saw my birds decoyed,
And then, bewitched, to shine
As candles round our Blessed Lady's shrine.

Oh Mary full of grace,
Oh Lily, incandescent offering,
Send forth Thy birds apace,
Send forth Thy birds to sing
The untold glories of thy endless Spring!

ii MADONNA OF THE WINTER FLOWERS

One iridescent day in deep December
Opal-soft and mild;
And darkling violets at the Incarnation
Of the heavenly Child:
The rain-filled rose anticipates the Spring,
And frankincense, a kingly offering.

She only knew, oh star-crowned Queen of Heaven,
The anguish of that birth:
The stain of blood-dark violets He would gather
From the sardonic earth:
Five-petalled rose, the mocking gift of Spring,
And bitter myrrh, that kingly offering.

MISCELLANEOUS POEMS
1954 – TO DATE

OXFORD TRINITY TERM 1954

On Magdalen Tower we wake the day
With wisps of music feather soft,
Madrigals which float aloft
To greet the chilly month of May.

Opulent in fitful June
Lilac and laburnum bloom
The crimson hawthorn and the white
North Oxford's rain washed streets delight.

Glaucous and slow the Cherwell creeps;
Oxford raves while Cowley sleeps.
At dead of night the saxophone
Enchants us with its pleasant moan.

Fox-trotting slowly, cheek to cheek,
We dance till dawn's first crimson streak;
Rotating swiftly, hand in hand
We waltz to Tommy Kinsman's band.

Barefoot on the sodden lawn
We wander whispering in the dawn.
My velvet dress is drenched with dew
My senses reel at touch of you.
Oh! Scholarship's a million miles away
In glorious June and radiant May.

Tommy Kinsman's band was the first choice for Commemoration Balls in Oxford and May Balls in Cambridge during the 1950s.

A VIEW OF THE POTTERIES

Derelict and desolate
Beneath a glowering sky
Thick with greasy effluent
The sullen Trent creeps by

The park is full of rubbish,
The furnaces are cold;
Where eggshell porcelain once was made
Now plastic tat is sold.

The park is full of paper,
The lake is full of tins;
The bottle kilns are home to rats
Which rootle through the bins.

The football team slips down the League,
The terraces are bare.
The dole queue stretches down the street
And shuffles round the square.

The statue of Josiah
Is smothered in birdlime
While potteries in South Korea
Grow rich on his design.

*   *   *

The road runs to Etruria –
Evocative the sign –
And all at once the Arno flows
Round Ashton-under-Lyme.

With orange groves in Burslem
And cypresses in Stoke,
The golden glow of Tuscany
Dispels the Midland smoke.

While shepherdess and satyr dance
On Hanley's pleasant plain;
The Trent flows clear till Wedgwood's dreams
Materialise again.

Walking from the Crown Court at Hanley to the railway station at Stoke-on-Trent – it must be one of the most depressing walks in Europe – I saw a road sign which read "Etruria". It fired my imagination.

LOVE ON THE SOUTHERN REGION

The women you approve of
They drink their gin in bars,
They fill their diaries months ahead
With Primrose League bazaars;
From Godalming to Haywards Heath
Compare their motor cars.

They walk right round at Walton Heath
With brisk respectful gait;
They read the Daily Telegraph
Regret Rhodesia's fate;
They talk about Jim Slater
(Though not so much of late)

The coalition that we planned
Is frail enough I know,
For you are off to Haywards Heath
And I am off to Bow
Your handicap where Bow Bells ring
Is not a thing to show

*Written in 1956, the year that Rhodesia
declared unilateral independence.
Jim Slater was Chairman of Investment Bank Slater
Walker which collapsed shortly afterwards.*

DAMAGE BARTON

The brook which cuts the mountainside
Decants into the secret bay;
The pebbles rattling in the tide
Fly landwards in the sparkling spray.

Above the tide, beyond the rocks,
Invisible among the trees,
The badger and the furtive fox
Pad softly through the fallen leaves.

Tucked in the elbow of the hill
Encircled by the gorse gold moor,
Immutable, it rests above
The terror of the Severn bore.

The ancient farmhouse vigil keeps,
Observes the channel where she sails
The little, gallant, storm-tossed ship
Past Mortehoe and the coast of Wales.

Where Severn and Atlantic meet
Look west and see where Lundy lies
Foursquare against the storm, to greet
The petrel tossed from furious skies.

The air is sweet with honeyed gorse,
The farmhouse sleeps above the bay;
The earth rotates its calm diurnal course
And snowdrops glimmer in the fading day.

Dedicated to Peter and Mary Lethbridge

DASH

From Aberdeen to Samarkand
I trot the silken way
I am my master's little dog
He speaks and I obey

From Samarkand to Dun Huang
With China in our sight
Past golden mosques and singing sands
Parched days and starry nights.

At Kiz Kurghan the captive girl
Embraced a demon King
I trotted past, I do not care
For such a trivial thing.

From Lashkar Gah to the Indus
The Macedonian's way
Where Alexander marched I'll trot
Forever and a day.

From Scotland to Afghanistan
I love him till I die;
And now we sleep in Kabul
United in the sky.

Sir Aurel Stein (1862-1943) archaeologist and scholar, spent a lifetime exploring the Silk Road and traced Alexander the Great's route to the Indus. He was always accompanied by his dog Dash, a Scots Terrier, who over a period of forty years, went through seven incarnations. Both died in Kabul and I like to think they are buried together.

TRANSGENERATIONAL
POEMS WRITTEN BY MY MOTHER
AND YOUNGEST GRANDSON.

FREDA Katharine Lethbridge 1904 – 2001.

THE SPRITE Caleb O'Connor written age 10

THE BATTLE OF HASTINGS Caleb O'Connor written age 12

FREDA
THIS LADY THAT I LOVED....

This lady that I loved
Enters the twilight, where my veiled eyes see
A person worn and proved
With greying hair and age bent poverty.
I'd weep to see her, but that this I know
All thither go

She turns once more to me
Against the woods alight with dying gold,
Spindle and dogwood tree,
Cadence of scarlet, crimson manifold
That fade to weariness and sodden lie
Bidding goodbye.

Naked the trees and grey
Afresh with moss, bereft of leaf and cold
Where she goes eagerly
Under a frail moon poised, star-struck and bold
And in her hand outheld at this dark hour
A crescent flower.

This poem was written by my mother, Katharine Lethbridge, née Maynard, on the death of her own mother Alfreda Maynard, née Eppes, of Appomattox Manor, Virginia, USA.

THE SPRITE

The Sprite at first glance looked like a bumble bee
It turned out to be something much different.
Its body, shadowed by black but poisoned with yellow.
The face was in dazzling brightness as the
yellow slowly consumed its body
The see-through wings allowed any human
to look into their future.
The legs consumed by shadowed blackness were
slimy like a creature from a far dark planet.
Brown legs like twigs fallen from nature's wooden statue.
Black pointy ears like elves' but stolen and
now corrupted by darkness
They are like the sharpest spear taken from their previous owners.
A collar of poisoned yellow fur like a wolf.
It asserts its place in a higher order.

THE BATTLE OF HASTINGS

They stand alone on their hill.
As arrows fly against their will.
The invaders march ever closer.
And so do their soldiers

Suddenly the wall breaks
As the enemies retreat in a fake.
Down goes the Anglo-Saxon rack
As the Norman axes hack.

And now off they go to heaven
Dead due to Norman aggression.

EPILOGUE

NATIVITY

How far east of Eden rose the Star
Which spun through interstellar space?
Past parallax, across the shining bar
Which led the pious Magi to the place
Where shepherds watched, where ox and ass adore
The holy Babe and Mary full of grace.

Ecliptic zodiac, celestial file
Where asteroid and super nova spins
Pulsar and quasar light the holy mile
Where universe completes and time begins,
Exultant bells ring out through endless space
Announce the Child and Mary full of grace

How small the stable and how thin the straw
The manger narrow as a tomb,
How chill the wind which sweeps the stony floor
And swirls the dust around the darkened room.
The gentle beasts bear witness to the birth
The benison which melts the frozen earth.

So vast the universe, the countless stars
Where Cepheid and Gas Giant roll,
How strange that Earth, the smallest of them all
Should halt the Star captivate the soul.
Appropriate the animals should see Him first
Omega and Alpha, last and first.

REFLECTION

I would like to dedicate the last poem to Professor Brian Cox. In his television series "Universe" he wonders why, in the vast celestial landscape, while a few of its occupants may be capable of sustaining some simple amoeba-like forms of life, only one, as far as we know, planet Earth, is rich in the diversity of the life it sustains.

I, for myself, wonder why, with such celestial variety at His disposal, the Saviour chose little Earth for His Incarnation.

ABOUT THE AUTHOR

Nemone Lethbridge

Born in India in 1932 to a military family with a long tradition of service to the Raj; Nemone Lethbridge was educated at Tudor Hall School and Somerville College, Oxford. One of two girls in her year to read law she was told by a (male) tutor that the idea of a woman going to the Bar was ludicrous. Nevertheless, she was called in 1956, one of a tiny handful of women to achieve this. Many doors were closed to these few: work was hard to come by. It was lucky chance that Nemone became counsel of choice for the notorious Kray Twins.

PRAISE FOR AUTHOR

This book is absolutely brilliant. *****

Unputdownable extraordinary story *****

*A cracking story***** *What a story (or set of stories). Taking you from India to the slums of Kilburn via post-war Germany and a hushed up naval disaster, it is a cracking good read.*

- AMAZON REVIEWS OF NEMONE

BOOKS BY THIS AUTHOR

Nemone: A Young Woman Barrister's Battle Against Prejudice, Class And Misogyny. Her Controversial Marriage. (Nemone Lethbridge)

Born in India in 1932 to a military family with a long tradition of service to the Raj; Nemone Lethbridge was educated at Tudor Hall School and Somerville College, Oxford. One of two girls in her year to read law she was told by a (male) tutor that the idea of a woman going to the Bar was ludicrous. Nevertheless, she was called in 1956, one of a tiny handful of women to achieve this. Many doors were closed to these few: work was hard to come by. It was lucky chance that Nemone became counsel of choice for the notorious Kray Twins, a position that she occupied for seven years.In 1959 she married Jimmy O'Connor whose background from a poverty-stricken Irish family was the polar opposite of her own. This marriage outraged the establishment: In 1942 Jimmy had been convicted of murder and sentenced to death. That sentence was commuted to one of life imprisonment. He was released on license in 1952 and became what a leading critic called "perhaps the most important writer to come out of prison since Bunyan". Nevertheless, the Bar turned its back on Nemone, and it took eighteen years for her to find Chambers where she could resume her professional practice.

Printed in Dunstable, United Kingdom